WATER

John Akhilomen

WATER
Copyright © 2018 by John Akhilomen

John Akhilomen
jonbasanti@gmail.com

ISBN: 978-1986802369
ISBN-13: 1986802361

DEDICATION

Dedicated to my parents (Helen & Samuel); daughter (Chenya); fiancé (Gabriela), siblings (Sammy, Paul, and Gladys); Sister-in-law (Bidemi), other parents (Maria, Lee & Hector), nieces (Kasharyea, Kamaryea, Kari & Joy). And to all believers of what is good and right keep believing and I hope that you find that which you seek.

Table of Contents

HEAT

VAPOR

FROZEN

A SPECIAL DEDICATION TO THE READER

Preface

I think I wrote my first poem when I was 11 years old. I had written a love-letter on behalf of my elder brother and addressed it to a girl he wanted to woo while back in junior high school. Thenadays when we were kids, writing love-letters or love-lyrics to the girls was how we could get their attention. Thus, I picked up the nickname "love-letter". I didn't just write on behalf of my elder brother, I also wrote on behalf of his friends and my friends as well.

It wasn't until I was 14 years old I was introduced to the world of poetry. When I was in senior high school, I had a friend who had dyslexia and wrote poems. I can recall seeing my first poem the day I was in his classroom to pick him up for lunch which was a few blocks away from mine, we often ate lunch together. He was focused on a piece of paper he was writing upon, he wasn't even aware I was around. Recalling that day now, I was experiencing for the first time, the making of a poem which was beautiful. He finished his writing and surprisingly tossed away the piece of paper he had written upon. Curiously I picked it up and read what he had written upon it, it was so beautiful that it made me teary-eyed.

Fast forward many months later I was converting my love-letters to poems. Later in my life, I would go on to study English poets like (John Keats, William Shakespeare, William Wordsworth, William Blake). I wrote poems and shared with a few trusted friends back then.

Thus I became a poet. I used to think of what that meant, being a poet. Poets don't just write poems, they use the power of words to paint them. Poets paint poems with words. And a well-crafted poem can transcend the reader to that emotional state which the poem is conveying. That was what I became when I said I became a poet. I became a painter with words. Whenever I craft a poem, I always hope to transcend the reader to the state of emotion which the poem conveys.

As an insane poet, I have harnessed both feminine and masculine energies within myself to weave each line that's crafted the poems in the anthology Water, romanticizing the longing for love as well as its cosmic extension between both energies.

I have chosen Water as the title of this anthology because I want the readers to resonate with the emotions of Joy, Romance, Healing, Eroticism, Hope, Longing conveyed separately like a river flowing through an experience of Love. My philosophy is quite a simple one; Love is the essence of our being as human beings. I believe Love is our sole purpose and destiny. My concept of Love is a cosmic extension between the male and female energies. When the male and female energies are harmoniously joined together in perfect balance, they create this "Oneness" which is the true essence of God, like in this poem shown below:

When you and I
are like this

despite what people say

is
the simplest image
of God.

Love can truly be experienced when we become like water. To
know how beautiful the world is underwater, we need to immerse
ourselves in it. The feeling of being wet in the rain is a different
feeling from being wet underwater. However, both feelings are
resonated by water. We can only immerse ourselves in Love to
experience it. Love can't be defined. Through Love, we can
experience union. Through Love, we can know our selves and
others. This powerful collection of poetry by John Akhilomen will
take you through an experience of different essential characteristics
of the feminine and masculine spirit. The poems in this book have
been grouped by four chapters; Fluid, Heat, Vapor, and Frozen.

WATER

I light my own fire
from inside me.

The power of creation
is
in Love.

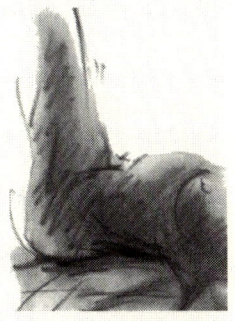

Between sheets
her body sang
an erotic music
that erupted
a fiery passion
inside his heart,
and he couldn't
get enough
of that sassy
and sexy rhythm;
her breast looked delicious to eat
her perfect lips like heaven to kiss
her neck, thighs, and backside
were just perfect the way they were.

-Between sheets

FLUID

As for Love,
it will
burn you
in that
huge arch of colors
that flaunts
across the sky,

and leave you like that.

-What Love does

Admire yourself
like the Moon does
with the lake.

-Admire yourself

I haven't been kissed nor held
in a long while,

Said the poor old man
whom Life had already left alone
to such unfriendly Sadness.

Then took him in her arms of Love
the little girl
and wept.

This is what it feels like
when the Universe kisses you
and holds you.

And he smiled
when Life came back to him

-*The Little Girl*

Art, itself
is the Beauty
of God,
and the artist
can paint God well.

-Art

If you open my book
of love poems,

God said,

you will find
that it begins with you
and ends with you.

-My book of love poems

God
and I are
like two waters
of love that'd merged
to become one large ocean.

-One large ocean

God is complete
if I can wrap you
inside me
like this.

-Untitled

Look at us,

we are all
colorful appearances
of the divine.

-Untitled

When you and I
are like this
despite
what people say

is
the simplest image
of God.

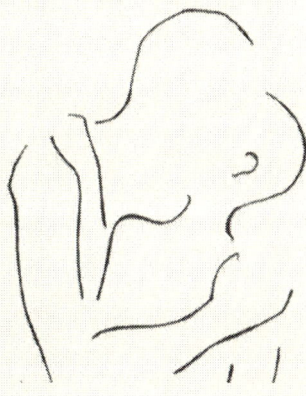

-The simplest image of God

One thing I know for sure my darling
is that;

you're
the other half
of my whole Universe,

and I'm
the other half
of your whole Universe,

and together like this
we're
a single Universe.

-A Single Universe

I
am you
looking back
at my own Light.

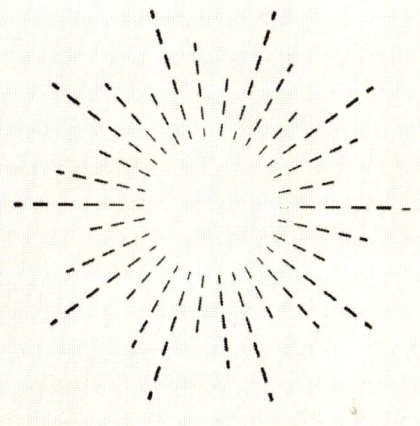

-Light

If you can truly
know yourself

then you can
truly know me too.

-Untitled

In the pool of wine
everything good and evil
is shamelessly drunk.

-Untitled

As for
what God could be,
I guess
anything as Light and Shadow
laughing together in harmony.

-What God could be

I found **God**
more in

what I am
than
who I am.

-Untitled

This is my Truth:

all my I's come together
to fuse the actions
in my being as
I am.

-My Truth

I'm always in a dream
I know it

whether I'm awake
or asleep.

-Always in a dream

Love is
our union,
you and I.

Love binds every
this and that
of us together.

We are together
in Love.

-Love is our union

Come into my arms
most-beautiful one,

I want to wrap you
inside them
like a gift of stars,

and make you shine
like the whole universe.

-A gift of stars

Let Love guide you on
the right path and
you shall find
that which
you seek.

-The path of Love

Love in the end
will lead us all
through the stairways
of heaven,
even the ones
ignorant of what Love is.

-Love in the end

You
are the
house of Love
where God resides
and inside this house,
God keeps everything you seek.

-The house where God resides

Inside this house,
beautiful and elegant
creatures reside,
and they are always
dialoguing in harmony.

-Inside this house

Sing to me of the past
of sweet and caressing times
of timeless wonders
of budding youths
of arrogant wars
of the night stars

of the mysterious lady
you saw written on my palm
of the barking dog
in the wilderness
of the happy seas and
changing clouds
sing to me
how my mother became yours.

Sing to me
a song of my birth
a song of hope
a song of freedom
a song of spring
a song of bravery.
Sing to me.

-Sing to me

Never give up.
From one door to another
keep knocking
until you find that
which you seek.

-Untitled

You are the Miracle
you've been long looking for.
Whatever emotion **Water** can flow with
you can too.
Whatever passion **Fire** can burn
you can too.
However light-weight **Air** can be
you can too.
Whatever garden the **Earth** can plant
you can too.

-Untitled

Look at Water
and see how large it is,
deep,
yet can be small
if need be.
Flow like Water does
and Life will deliciously
soak your breast.

-Water is large

Let it be for dancing
we have come here.

Let it be for kissing
you have called me out
in the rain.

Let it be for you
that I exist.

Let it be for Love
you have come
all this way
to see my face.

-Let it be

Only with your own Beauty,
can you describe
the beauty
in others.

-*The Beauty in others*

You with whom
I have dreamed my whole life with,
I love you with my all my dreams
from childhood.

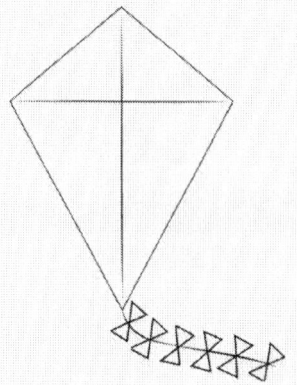

-Dreams from Childhood

WATER

HEAT

Fall in love
and light up the
whole earth and sky
from inside you

-Fall in Love

God lights you
into existence with Love.

Won't you
light up
this world
for us
with your Love?

-Light up this world

For as long
as I am with you
my sweetheart

I'm home
wherever I am.

-I'm home

He looked at me
with shining eyes
and said,

*You are
the most beautiful
flower-garden
that exist*

*and I appreciate
every flower
that grows from inside you.*

That's how amazing he's,
my man.

-My man

Because of how
she was beautifully made

I could look at her
just once

and fell in love with her.

-She

He lit
the whole universe
inside her
with just one kiss.

-One Kiss

To me
Helen is
a thing of beauty
and wonder.

I saw her the first time
when I opened my tiny eyes,
she had folded me in her arms,

like a flower
I'd blossomed
in the warmth
of Helen.

-To Helen

I like your rough hands
on my body

like this

makes me insanely
wild for you.

-Insanely wild

I want
to drench your
Body in this Wine
and sip you bit by
bit and slowly while
I have the whole
night making
love
to
You.

-Untitled

When you kiss me
like this,

like that
I go insane
and I unsettle
myself.

When you touch my breast
like that,

like this
I go wild
and I untrust
myself.

When you whisper in my ears
like this,

like that
I go quiet,

under the spell
of your voice
I am vulnerable.

-Like this, Like that

I opened my legs
the way he liked it
and strangled them inside my skirt
and his lazy hands were everywhere
inside, touching me anywhere, anyhow
here and there and everywhere
until he flamed me up
inside.

-Untitled

He undressed her gently,
he had the whole night
and he was patient.

He ate her hairs
and gnawed at the best
places he touched,

and licked her breast and
gnawed at them too,

and all of him
was inside her,
taking her apart.

She liked him inside her
that way,
creaming her entire.

There was no part of her he missed
and went through every corner of her,

and yes
he was passionate,
too passionate
he made her insane,

made her want more and
more he gave,
more,
until she spilled all over
like wine.

He kept the wildflower
in his arms
and spooned
her.

-He

Sing and laugh with me still
the Moon said,
I am drunk
and my head is not right.
Kiss my lips once more,
tonight, what I want
is you.

There is passion
soaking out of my delicious breast yet,
she said,
come closer
and touch them.

Anything about you
drives me mad,
even the way
you're made
seduces me.

I have
adorned myself only for you
and tonight, what I desire
is you.

-The moon and I

I like it
whenever you mishandle
my breast like this,

it ignites my whole body
for sex.

-Mishandling

She liked
how her skin felt with his,
her body under his.

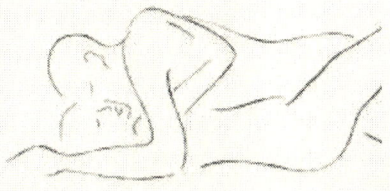

He liked
the taste of her
dripping body
and she liked the
taste of his.

She liked her body wrapped
inside his body
while they made love

he, kissing this and that
of her,
folding and unfolding
her body
and enjoying
to the slow music
of it

she, liking
him inside her
crushing her bones,
breathing her soul for it,
liking her smell inside him.

-She liked.

She took a rope and tied
herself to him

and said

*Look, now I shall forever be
inside your chest*

and you shall never leave me.

He looked at her
and laughed.

*it's I
my dear,*

*I had tied and knotted the rope,
and now
that I am inside your chest
you shall never leave me.*

*You are
my breadth
and
I'm your head.*

-She

She
was made
for me
to love
for the
rest of
my life.

-She

You are the only
beautiful thing

that exist
I know of

and every fiber
of my being

is
in
love
with
you.

-Beautiful thing

Every imaginable self
of me
I can imagine,

numberless form
of me
I can think of,

possibility
for me,

will
always
love you.

-Every possibility for me

To
Love is
our destiny,
you
and
I.

-Our destiny.

I have looked
into your eyes
and seen
every dream
I am,

He said to her.

-Untitled

I love you

I love you mentally

I love you far beyond
reasons physicals

I love you far beyond
expressions which
make any sense.

-I love you

She wore a million stars
on her face
like smiles

because tonight
he had kissed her
on her lips.

-She.

A cold night
like this one,

my body seeks your body
to wrap itself with

-She.

I love you more
than I love you.

I love you with the least
and best
of me.

-I love you more

To *love me,*

she said,

is to
look at me
and see yourself
as I am.

-She

Look at her
once again
and see
that her beauty
is in her
Smile.

-Her smile.

I'm contented
with the
crazy
genuine
and divine
ways I love you

my heart's heart
soul's soul
my heaven.

-My everything

Since I saw her beautiful face,
I haven't been able
to gather together
everything that makes her
this
amazingly beautiful.

-Her beautiful face

The Sun does this
to the ocean every time
he rises
in the morning:

He excites her
with lots of kisses.

-The Sun does this to the ocean

Love
binds all my existences
into just one;

the beginning,
middle way,
and ending.

-One existence

My sweetheart,
with this diamond ring, I wed you
with all I am,

senseless
fenceless
in
my love for you,

mindless
anything less
in
my desire for you,

where you and only you
luxuriate this
that I with you wed
with all of me.

-Wedding poem

I am Love
your mother,
destiny,

I have kissed
the moon,

flirted with the stars

and everything
dances
to the rhythm
of my body.

In my presence
all intentions dissolve
into one dance.

- Mother Love

I shall fight hard
what I am not.

What I am not
is the shadow of my Light

and to pick up
my dreams like stars
I need my own Light
to see where they are
in the sky.

-Fight to win.

Every

second in a minute
minute in an hour
hour in a day,
I think of you.

I do nothing most
but love and miss you
the same time
my darling.

-Love and miss you

You are all that

my heart can murmur,

mind can wonder,

soul can dream,

and everything I am

you are,

and everything you aren't

I'm not.

-Untitled

I want a haven,
someplace I can hide away
and forget everything I once knew,

said the man,

I want to be born-again
you know, that newborn child
from the union of
Water and Fire,
smells fresh, pleasant eyes,
a new body that burns
and never gets old,
stays a child forever.
And my hair won't even be this difficult to comb
nor my skin this hard.
I'm tired of being known
I want to be the unknown
the forgotten one,
a stranger
to even myself,
the mother that bore me,
and the father I esteem.

-Born Again

I know that
in my beginning
the Divine formed you and me
separately from a Union of Love,
so that
you and I alone comprehend
the mystery of our Love.

-In My Beginning

WATER

VAPOR

I have seen myself
to know what I am.

I cannot limit it
to a name or identity,
a religion, nationality or gender.
I cannot limit it
to me even.

-Limitless

Do not ask me
who I am;

anything I tell you
would be a lie,
I cannot comprehend
what I am.

When I say,
I am,
is not the same
when I say,
I.

-

I,
extends everything I can assume
yet the reality of it all
is just what I am,
a single extension
of every assumption
in my Light or Shadow;

including the stars
brimming in the night skies,
and next to the stars above
wears my face
like the enchanting moon,
the ocean, horizon,

and every morning,
wears my face above
like the beautiful sun,
leaving gold dust
on the Earth's nappy hair,

before birth, childhood,
adulthood, beyond death,
yet just one single existence
when I say,
I am,
began from nowhere,
ends nowhere,

keeps the
union of
my Bodies and Soul
together in one place,
as River is,
Ocean,
Rain,
Spring

and
the fountain
keeping the
Tree of Life
alive in the
garden of Eden,

and I,
dances
sings
laughs many,
yet just in one singles existence,
every laugh I'd laughed
song I'd sung
dance I'd danced
pain I'd felt
tears I had cried,

that
I too
can arise
leaping myself
to touch
the soft face of God
beyond every reality,
knowing that
God first and last
binds to only me.

When I say,
I am,
binds together
all the dreams of me
into just one dream,
where I,
extends every dream

my soul dreams.

Do not ask me
who I am,
I cannot
comprehend it,

but
look through me instead
and behold all
my faceless faces

and see that
Love keeps them all
in just one

and all my dreamless dreams,
together in just
one dream.

-I, I am

I flapped my arms
like wings
leaped and flew
because that's
what birds do.

-My arms like wings

Do the stupidest thing
that makes you laugh
and make God laugh too,

dance like an idiot
if you must.

When you dance
God dances too.

-Make God dance too

When I was a little boy,

I flew
because my father's arms
were strong.

I bloomed like
a flower
because my mother's kisses
were delicious
with Life.

-When I was a little boy

I see God scattering
genie-lamps all over
the earth like
stars.

-Genie lamps

Spring is coming,
bring your pitcher
and start it now,
don't wait,

and watch how it blooms
when spring comes.

-When Spring comes

I am
the most beautiful
garden
that is

and Love
is my gardener.

-My Gardener

Believe me
I've got wings

and like the birds
I too can fly.

For me though,
the sky is not the limit.

-I can fly

Ahah!

Now
watch me
paint my dreams
in the sky like

rainbows.

-Dream painter.

Look at how high
a bird can fly,

that's what Hope
does with its feathers,

takes it farther
to the sky.

And listen to it sing,
it does not care who listens,
it just sings.

-Feathers

smile there is.
the brightest
dazzling with
me
see
and
sky
the
in
up
Look

.

-Brightest smile

Your talents are like rainbows,

paint the world!

Your words are like gold,

bless the world!

-Talents and Words

We have all been marked
for something
marvelous
since childhood,

we are all
starborn.

-Starborn

Look inside your mirror
and smile
to yourself,

you will find
that
the only
beautiful face
in there

is yours.

-Inside your mirror

sky
the   and
to   down
up
Look

to know
your measure

if even you are
unaware
of it.

-Your measure

The garden of Eden
you are
and your gardener
is God,
and inside you
has planted the
Tree of Life
and the
Tree of Wisdom
separately.

-Untitled

Laugh!

Your face
is mysteriously beautiful
whenever you do,
and your flowers open
because of your sunlight.

Dance!

Your body
is mysteriously sensual
whenever you do,
and the universe unfolds itself
upon your hip
because of your
mystical appearance.

-Your sunlight and appearance

As for man,

the air
he breathes.

The fire
keeps him alive.

The Earth and Water
vessels him.

-As for man

Let me let you in
on a little secret:

your soul is an
amazing
universe
and every star
part of it
is a unique dream.

-Amazing

Little April came to him
in a dream
and wore a bangle of cowries
on his wrist

She said,
time is coming to us, friend.
Protection, protection my friend!
and smiled.

She wrapped him in her arms,
warmed him up from the terrible cold,

I am here now!
she said
and smiled,

she opened his eyes to many things
said many things to him
showed him magic
wiped his tears
and made him laugh

Come with me, friend,
she said

I'll take you
to Neverland
and you shall be safe
there with me.

She took him upon her wings
and flew him away.

-Mother fairy

The Face of Love is
the most handsome face
any man can wear

and the most beautiful face
any woman can wear,

said the son of man
on the mountaintop.

Wear your face
handsomely
and beautifully
like the face of Love.

-The Face of Love

So, I met
Jesus the man from Galilee
returning from Jerusalem
after the crucifixion
and asked him,

What advice do you have for me,
O son of man?

The same I gave Magda a while ago,
He said,

Express your self!

And continued his way
laughing.

-The Man from Galilee

Look at me, Magda,

Said Jesus,

I am a better dancer.

And bent his waist
like this
and twisted his hips
like that
and danced
and God came out laughing.

-Look at me Magda

I had a dream last night,
it was Jesus
dancing.

I asked him,

O Son of Man,
what does this mean?

He said,

I am the dancer
and God is the dancing.

-Jesus dancing

Please pour me more wine,
said I to the wine-bearer.

I like it when I'm like this;
I can be sitting beside God and
making the most boring joke
and God won't stop laughing.

-Drunkard

I looked through
the Son of man
and beheld
my beautiful face alone.

-Untitled

Who dreams
when you're asleep,
She asked me.

I said me.

Who dreams
when you're awake,
She asked me.

I said me.

Who is dreaming now?

It is I,
said me,

I am the dreamer and
the dreaming.
I dream you as
you dream me.
The eye in which
we dream each other
is the same.

-Dreaming

Inside
my Self
I see
Heaven
and Earth
existing
only
as one
Union
in all.

-Heaven and Earth

Two men went inside the temple
to offer their sacrifices to God.

Wept the first one:
O God,
have pity on this poor old fellow,
I have been all day with neither bread
nor wine, nor honey,
a weak feebled hunger,
broken lips, weatherbeaten,
if only I can find
a small piece of bread to eat.

Then wept God,
Yes.

Then went one to bake bread
while another went to the vineyard
to make wine.
And another went to brew
hop and barley to mild.

Then continued the poor old fellow,
O God,
a small piece of bread is enough even.

Wept God again,
Yes.

Then stopped the brewing and making
and accepted his sacrifice,
and he went away crying.

Meanwhile Laughing the second one:
Thank you, O God,
I'm a fine baker of bread,
a drunk brewer of hop and barley,
a fine maker of wine,
the beekeeper of the entire honeycomb
from your beehive.

Then laughed God
Yes.

I'm part of everything
everything is part of me,
and I'm part of you.

Your head is the Air
your body is the Water
your foot is the Earth
and your spirit is the Fire
and all together
you're God.

Laughed God again,
Yes.

My body is Earth and Water
My Soul is Fire and Water
and all together
I'm mankind
and you and I together
is a single appearance of
what Love is.

Laughed God again,
Yes.
And accepted the sacrifice
of the drunken fellow,
and he went away laughing.

-Two men went inside the temple.

They had sat on a huge rock by the river.
Basanti pulled up a wrecked shoe like a fish.

Sam.

Don't cast it back,
the shoe's mine.
It had come back to me
after all these years
and you finding it means something.
When last I saw this shoe
was around your age,
I'd gone fishing one evening
with my father when this river
stole it from me
and gave back my father's shawl.

Basanti.

What does this mean?

Sam.

The last sayings of my father
has walked its own way
to you,
an ageless spirit
passed down,
and I must speak.

Basanti.

Speak to me father.

*Sam took Basanti by his right hand and
walked him home.*

Sam.

They were brave ones
who died in the war,
great men and women,
rebels who had come and gone,
died for the cause of Love,
died for the betterment
of all mankind,
buried them
like warrior poets,
erected long statutes for them.
Yet much hasn't changed.
But the watercourse
of all actions
must go on.

And Life, son,
is a book of many pages.
There are sadder
than happy ones.

Know this and you'll be well with it:
when God's face to face with you
Its Light fall on you.
When God's back faces you
Its shadow falls on you.
Both Light and Shadow
is all God's,
and the right to choose
any identity is all yours.

Whenever you see the rain,
laugh with it and dance too.
Laugh in the moonlight and dance too.
Whenever you hear the birds sing
sing with them,
flap your arms like wings
and thrust like them too.
Everything is a part of you
and you're a part of everything.

Basanti.

What's my destiny?

Sam stopped. Took Basanti's palms and read them.

Love is your sole destiny son.
There's a beautiful lady
in the distance

coming your way.
When she comes,
spoil her with kisses
and give her the best of your stars
because she'll be your moonlight.

She'll give you beautiful children,
love them with all your heart.

They continued their journey home.

Your mother bore you with Love,
love her with all your heart too.
Break your body for her sake if you must
and what comes from it
let it be hers.

And God, son,
is the sole experience,
has hidden nothing
from the soul
and known only
to the soul
which experiences It
in itself.
But what is the Soul
but your self
and what's your self

if not that Love
without any appearance
keeps everyone inside the Godhead
in perfect balance with the other.
And you have been made in Its image they say
is a mysterious and complex being.

Never forget that Fear
is the shadow of your Light,
and when you don't
know yourself.

Know yourself,
and dream on.
Life is but a dream,

*A week later, Basanti stood alone wearing one shoe and
looked up to the skies.*

Basanti.

He said many things to me that day
my father and
died the next morning.
He was a warrior poet,
he lived like one,
and we buried him like one.

-The Shoe

He was standing front his mirror
looking for
cute faces,
costumes,
he once wore.

They were no longer there
where the old man
was standing now.

His curls
had straightened up short,
he had lost much of his hairs.
He stood there yesterday
where he was standing now;
a heap of used-coals
could never be this grayer.

Looking back,
yesterday was better,
he thought.
He had himself plenty candies and floss,
nothing he ever did was right or wrong,
the world was fiction then.
He blamed no one for a broken limb
and liked anything that looked like a rainbow.
Now nothing's like it used to be,
and he wished he hadn't died.

-Changes

I too
am my own friend.

I too
am my own enemy.

-I too.

These delightful flowers
are dancing,

please stay quiet for a moment,

I want to listen to
their dance.

There is a mystery in their dance
I want to learn,

that sensual movement
which mesmerizes me.

Please stay quiet for a moment

and listen,

listen to what makes me cry.

-When flowers dance.

Anytime you see
the sun kissing the earth
like this, that I am.

-I am

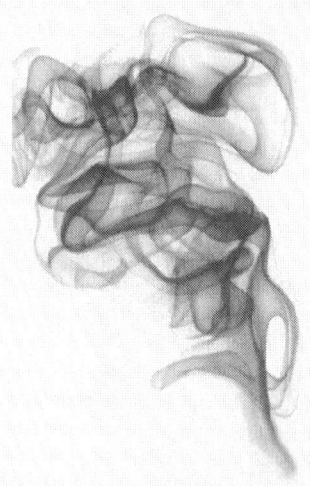

That which
is unknown
dancing awkwardly
to touch God
on the face
I am.

-I am

I 'm water,

life comes
from my breast.

-I 'm water

If you can put away
one after another
everything you think you are,

you will find that
a deep void of space
is what's left;
you!

-Untitled

I'm too unwise to understand
this:

Sometimes my soul makes a joke and I
hear God laughing.

Sometimes God is the music
my soul is dancing to.

Sometimes God would say:
Sit beside me and let me show you
how we had made the whole universe.
And I would see my soul
pretending to be God
and laughing at me.

Sit beside me and let me show you
how we had contained the whole universe
inside this house,
sometimes God would say,

and how we had painted the dream
of Maya outside of man.

Once I saw my Soul whispered
in God's ears
and heard between them:

Yes, that is our little secret,

that Love binds you to me.
(and me to you),

and whatsoever you are,
(that I am too),

and that which I am
(you are too).

-God and My Soul

Everyone I have met
has mistaken me for
something else I am not,

said the little boy
in his prayer to God,

and I'm sad
because me
no one knows.

And God said,

Even I.
I have been called
many names
I'm not,

been referred to as
many strangers
I'm not.

Don't be sad
most-beautiful one;
you and I alone
is enough.

In my solitude

I had a love dream last night,

it was your face,

and you had kissed me
on my lips.

Yet when they asked me
what your face was like,
I could not describe it.

Even
to myself,

I could not comprehend
our Romance.

-Love dream

This was what it meant
when Magda kissed Jesus's foot
and anointed them with her hair:
Love had occupied her soul
and he had become her love-sanctuary.

This was what it meant
when the dancer ripped her gown apart
in madness and danced:
she was in the presence of her handsome lover
and his eyes had shone with Love.

This was what it meant when I kissed
my dying father on his lips:
that Love's always between souls.

This was what it meant
when Mary was amazed
at the face
of Jesus on the cross:
she had seen the face of God,
he's always in Love.

-The meaning

Yesterday my head and chest
were together dancing inside one dance
and I saw inside this dance
three selves of my Self

Hurry and come!
Whispered one
in my ear,
Come and see!

What?
I chuckled,

and pulling me
by my hand
said the second one

*Come and see
the most-handsome one dancing
inside this Temple of Love.*

Then said the third one
*Listen to me,
you are the music
everything is dancing to.
Now, whatsoever you ask
shall be given to you.*

Then said the first and
the last,

*In this dancing we created
the whole universe again
and again.*

-Three selves of my self

Last night
with the moon's flamboyance
as the stars held up
their tiny lanterns to her face,
I had braided my hair
and adorned myself with pearls
and went up the hill to meet my Love
in the secret garden
no one knows.

My foot chimed
the rhythms of my heart
on each step
as I walked on
and my heart's contents
were only love verses.

Look at you, you are flushed!

Said the tall handsome tulip
who stood alone
guarding the entrance gate
of the garden

*Tonight, I go to the one I love
and he awaits me,*
I said.

*I see too much Love in your eyes
most beautiful-one,*

and the whole Universe
lights up from inside you,
He said,

Only with such beauty can
Love be revealed to us.

Go and be kissed
your Love's been
eager for you all day.

-The Tall Handsome Tulip

In a dialogue
Said I:

*What was it
had I been seeking all this time?*

*Had I been seeking your kingdom?
Or my Self?*

and God said

*When you seek your Self
you find my kingdom.*

*When you seek my kingdom
you find your Self.*

-Seeking the kingdom of God

Listen and dance,
it is your heart
that sings.

Dance
and light up
the whole Universe
for us.

-Listen and dance

You are like a tree,
you shed all your leaves
when it's winter
looking as though
the devil had just bedded with you.

And when it's spring
you bloom in fresh leaves
looking as though
God had just kissed
your delicious lips.

-The changing seasons.

You have really
not seen me dance,

the mad dancer said.

Whenever I do,
it's an explosion of Love
that can't be contained
everywhere

-*The mad dancer*

The whole universe
folds itself,
from inside you,
and unfolds itself
back again,
from inside you.

-Untitled

A man ran out of his house
one midnight and screamed

Thank you, O God,
because I cannot stay
happy every time.

-Untitled

I
know
how the sun
rises inside me
and how the sun sets
inside me;
It'
s
a
secret!

-Untitled

Anytime I whisper to my Self
I love you
God climbs down from
inside my heart
and kisses me
and whispers back to me
I love you too.

-Anytime I whisper to myself

Sometimes I'd sit alone
at night
and wonder
what if through dreams
I can transcend
all the lives I am living
right now
and see what
I really am.

-Untitled

Sometimes you look at me
and wonder
why I can't be normal
once even;

it's because Love has flirted with me
and we had many times done
insane things together.

Sometimes you try to listen to me
and you wonder
why I make no sense
to anyone;

it's because to God alone
I make a lot of sense.

Sometimes you wonder
why the moon always fascinated me
anytime we walked together
by this lake;

it's because I have kept
her ravishing face
inside my chest.

Sometimes you wonder what it meant
when I said
the whole universe is
the most beautiful piece of poetry
I ever heard
and God was the Poet.

Sometimes you wonder why
I would say things like
I live in the wildest memories
of all my selves,
the shameless whore I'm,
won't stop thinking about
those hot kisses
and wild love-making
we all had together.

Sometimes you wonder
how I could dance less
when I'm happy
and dance more
when I'm sad;

it's because
when God and Satan

came together and
played a trick on Job
and blessed him with wealth
and impoverishment,
he gladly received both;
Health and sickness,
he gladly received both too.

Sometimes you wonder
what Christ means to me;

that Air, Fire, Water, and Earth
can all
be inside God
and Love
keeps every one of them
in balance
with the other.

-Sometimes You Wonder

Truth comes from nowhere
but the fountain of your own soul.
Your Soul
is the
Wisdom
of the whole Universe

-Where Truth Comes From

I have forgotten
many things about me
to become what I am.

Forgive me
if I don't answer
to the names
you call me now.

I choose my names
and answer only
to what I call myself:
Rainbow, Beauty, Shine,
Sunrise, Sunset,
even Universe.

-Answering only to me

FROZEN.

You ponder and ponder
day after day

wonder and wonder
night after night

on who you are

that you have missed
God passed by.

-Missed God passed by

It's you
that's in your way.

Get out
of your way

and let
all your dreams
finally become you.

-Get out of your way

You have not stopped uttering
since you came here

God said,

Please go away from us.

And shut the door in my face.
And while I was leaving

said

Do not come back to us
until you have become
a mystery to
even yourself.

-God was disappointed

You must know
what you want
or else
every time God passes by
you won't stop mumbling.

-You must know what you want

He remembered a
friend he once knew,
who went everywhere with him
hiding a dagger in his back hand.

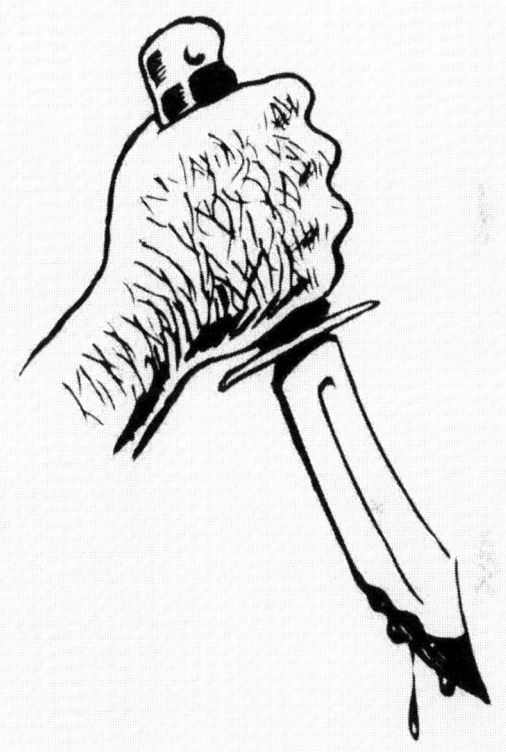

-He

He stood by his window niche
looking far away into the distance
for her silhouette
and wondering when next he'll
see her again.

His mind could think
nothing except her
and at night
when he closes his eyes
he could only dream of her
beautiful face.

Sometimes
he looked up in the night skies
and saw her smiles
filling the many skies with her soul
and the wind,
he liked how it pretended
to be her soft hands.

Sometimes when it's spring
all he could see around him
was her beauty
coloring the face of Spring.
And Spring smelled
like she smelled.

Tonight, like other nights
he's alone,
and he wonders if
tonight will be the night.

She was his heart's heart
soul's soul
his heaven
and he's not lived
since she left.

-He

The only time he saw a bright star,
he was a child,
his father carried him
on his wings
to reach for it;
when he couldn't reach any further,
his father stood taller
and he caught it like a dream.

The only time he laughed,
he was a child,
his father carried him in his arms
to fly,
carried him around and around
and said

flying bird,
reach beyond the skies!

And
he flew
flew
flew.

Nowadays he goes around
looking for that bright star,
that dream he once caught.
Anytime he leaped

to fly
he'd fall,
break a limb,
cry,
he was alone now
his father was long gone.

He saw him the last time,
kept in an opened box,
his face was disturbingly quiet
and masked like a ghost.

He's free now
little April said,

Come upon my wings
and I'll fly you
to a new dream.

-Broken

People always have a name for you
when you are not
what they want you to be:
Weird, Crazy, Dark,
Not one of us,
Stubborn.

-Untitled

One afternoon
I went to the flower garden
to meet my Love.

He sat amid the flowers
wondering why I had come.

I have so much to tell you,
I said to him

I have hidden myself from you
all this while
and I am ashamed.

Do not speak,
he quietly said
Do not say a word.

Come and sit beside me
and enjoy this peaceful moment
with me
my dear.

I felt ignored
and was grieved

Open your eyes,
I said
I love you, I really do.

He opened his eyes,
looked at me,
hesitated for a moment,
and said

*But your heart tells me
something different.*

-Untitled

Lazaro, there are many questions about *Why*
you ask me friend,
there are many things you want to know
but I have no answer to any.

Even I want to know,
I want to know many things,
who can tell me too?

I want to know why Night is dark
and Day is bright.
I want to know why there is you
and there is I;
every weeping sorrow that
comes with it
and the laughter it laughs.

I want to know you, Lazaro
I want to know about the seas
that go their untroubled distances,
where 'sit they go?
What do they carry with them?

The birds that flutter in the skies,
the ferry of the faraway distance to me,
and the little child that never speaks,
what 'sit she wants?

I want to know, why the dead?
What dreams do they go?

Are these whispers of midnight,
the talking spirits of my un-rested father?
I want to know the things they tell me
and which path they want to keep me from.
I want to know, why the changes?

There are many questions about *Why*
you ask me, my friend,
I have no answer to any.
Even I want to know
I want to know many things, Lazaro.

-Lazaro

It is what they do
I don't like,
things they say
about me,

when I'm there
when I'm not there,

fake noises
their eyes laugh,
counterfeit smiles
their tooth make,

when I'm there
when I'm not there.

-Untitled

For as long as there's war in heaven
there'll be a war on earth.
For as long as there's war within you
there'll be a war without you.

-Conflict

Don't be far gone
with this mask you wear
because it's not
what you are.
Become yourself
and you'll be such wonder
no one can ever dream of being.

-Become yourself

Speak up
when you must,
she said to her child,
and don't let your voice
be pulled down
by your trembling feathers.
Even the stupidest joke
can make the whole Universe
laugh out loud.

-Speak Up

Sometimes I wish
you can really
look at me and see your
self so that I won't exist even.

Said one man to another
and wept the other.

-Untitled

You whom had been born
a happy-go child
at the beginning of your day
should delight yourself
deliciously in the warmth of the tender sunrise
should refresh yourself
in the sophistication of the bracing sunset
should laugh aloud too
with the ocean's wave
your face should be enchanting
and your smile should brightly shine.

-You

A SPECIAL DEDICATION
TO THE READER

Act and Dance
like yourself.

Yes, God gives us
anything our heart
desires most and
we receive with
Faith and Patience.

Alas,
I crawled out of my skin
and hair
to become
what's underneath;
what I am.

Sometimes even a little Kindness
is enough.

Look around you,
there's got to be something
to be grateful for.

Nothing on Earth is owned.
Nothing will ever be owned.

The Light of your Soul
lights the whole Universe,
shine!

I, extends You
as
You, extends I;
we're One, You and I,
and Love alone can
unseparate Us.

Together God and I
bring things into existence
from nothing,

said my Soul to me one morning.

Dancing will take you farther
to the skies.

Have you discovered yet
how amazingly beautiful
your soul is?

When I looked
deep within myself
to know,
I found you
underneath.

Thank you for reading.

Acknowledgment

A deep appreciation to:

God, thank you for your eternal Love that extends all the lives I live as I am.

My darling mother Helen, thank you for being the best mother. Thank you for wrenching your back for us after father died. Thank you for all your Sacrifices and Love. Thank you for knowing and understanding me.

My late father Samuel, thank you for being the best father. Thank you for sacrificing your dreams for us. Thank you because in those 54 years you spent being our father, you showed me what father meant.

My fiancé Gabriela, thank you for your Love, Care, Affection, and Support. Thank you for being beautiful.

My esteemed brother Sammy, thank you for always being there for me in my darkest hour of need. Thank you for helping mom, Paul and I through those difficult years after father died. Thank you for your bravery and strength.

My kind Sister Gladys, thank you for all your Prayers & Support. Thank you for helping through Chenya's birth.

My other mother, the enchanting Magda, thank you for being a wonderful mother to me. Thank you for all your Prayers & Support.

Hector, thank you for all your Care & Support. You have been generous to me, and you're a wonderful father.

My brother Paul, my ravishing sister-in-law Bidemi, Femi & Ruth, thank you for all your prayers, appreciation and support.

All my followers on social media, thank you all for your kind support. A teddy-bear HUG from me.

And lastly, to my daughter Chenya, thank you for being the most beautiful girl in the world. Thank you for being an amazing daughter and thank you for choosing a dad like me 😊.

About the Author

John Akhilomen is a writer and poet with a style of poetry that is breathtakingly fresh, deep, and without boundaries. His ethereal poems continue to captivate the hearts of his huge online followers all over the world. Besides writing, John loves nature, traveling, art, reading, photography, and he is passionate about Love and a believer in what is good and right. He currently lives in Puerto Vallarta (a resort town on Mexico's Pacific coast) with his fiancé Gabriela.

Follow him online:

Facebook: @johnakhilomenwrites
Instagram: @johnakhilomen
Twitter: @JohnAkhilomen

Made in the USA
Columbia, SC
03 June 2018